Discovering Your Destiny

Dr. Shirley K. Clark

PURPOSE & DESTINY SERIES, VOL. 1

Dr. Shirley K. Clark
"Destiny Coach"

How to Release the Prophetic
Purpose of God to Operate in Your Life to
Secure Your Future

Discovering Your Destiny

Dr. Shirley K. Clark

Unless otherwise noted, scriptural quotations are taken from the King James Version of the Bible.

Discovering Your Destiny
(Formerly published under the title, "Warring With Your Prophetic Word")
Copyright © 2013
Shirley Clark International Ministries
www.drshirleyclark.org

Library of Congress — Cataloged in Publication Data

Printed in the United States

Ebook: 978-1-312-84931-0
Paperback: 978-1-312-84929-7
Hardback: 978-1-312-84930-3

Published by Jabez Books
(A Division of Clark's Consultant Group)
www.clarksconsultantgroup.com

All Rights Reserved. No part of this book may be reproduced or transmitted in any form or by any means, electronically or mechanically, including photocopying recording, or by any other information storage and retrieval system, without permission in writing from the publisher.

1. Purpose-driven 2. Destiny 3. Self-Esteem

Dedication

This book is dedicated to all my spiritual Fathers and Mothers that birthed me and poured into my life throughout my walk with the Lord.

- The Late Bishop Mack Timberlake, Jr. & Pastor Brenda Timberlake, Former Pastors

- Pastor Lawrence Turner, Spiritual Father

- Pastor Anne Logan, Intercessory Prayer Instructor

- Pastor Mark Chironna, Former Pastor

- Bishop T. D. & Serita Jakes, Current Pastors

- The Late Pastor Rupert Dudley, Evangelistic Trainer

- The Late "Mama" Tina Blakely, Crusade Trainer

- The Late Pastor Thomas Branch, Biblical Trainer

I am who I am because of all of these leaders. I am so very grateful to all of them!

Discovering Your Destiny

Thank You

- Thurman Clark, Jr. , My husband
- Family & Friends who supported me throughout this past year
- Patricia Scott, Copy Editor
- Cathy Johnson, Copy Editor

Other Books By

Dr. Shirley K. Clark

Pray & Grow Richer
Birthing Your Destiny
Living Your Destiny
Intercessors' Insights
Spiritual Warfare Teaching Manual and Workbook
The Ministry of Intercession
Prepare For War
Personal Spiritual Warfare
Pray, Push & Prevail
Strategic Warfare
The Midnight Cry
Empowering Your City
The Power of the "IF" Prayer Manual
52 Laws of Prayer

Table of Contents

Chapter 1
Your Destiny Await You   11

Chapter 2
Warfare is Inevitable   65

Chapter 3
Prospering in the Midst of Opposition   85

Chapter 4
What to Do When You Get a Prophetic Word   137

Chapter 5
A More Surer Word of Prophecy   197

Chapter One

Your Destiny Awaits You

The foundations of most Christian belief systems rest upon the basic concepts of the ultimate intentions and purpose of God.¹ Therefore, fulfilling of any future advent of prophecy that relates to our lives will always germinate from the womb or mind of God. Whatever God needs, he supplies it. Whatever God asks for, He answers it. Whatever God demands, He commissions it.

Prophecy is imminent. Throughout scripture when prophecy was used as a means to communicate the plan of God for an individual, there was stimulation of provocation. The prophecy would release a chain of reactions in both, the spirit and cosmic world that would lend itself to the fulfilling of it.

> *Often people look for deliverance to come from the outside or from external factors when going through adversity, but God has already placed a way of escape within our bowels.*

When we talk about God having a purpose and destiny for an individual's life, we are saying that God has predetermined a certain thing to happen. There is a motion of unknown occurrences for it to happen. And it is this "unknown" thing that often attracts unsolicited warfare and opposition in our lives. But just as it attracts adversity, the power to deliver is within it also. I heard Bishop T. D. Jakes, who is a renowned international speaker; say it this way, "God will deliver you through the thing you birth." The life of Moses is evidence of this. Moses' mother never conceived that the thing she was carrying inside of her was going to be the thing that would deliver her.

Often people look for deliverance to come from the outside or from external factors when going through adversity, but God has already placed a way of escape within our bowels. Our deliverance is within our belly. It is within our destiny. Concepts, dreams and ideas are conceived within, not without. And because of this, the greatness of God is constantly kicking within us "to be delivered."

Seeds of greatness

When we are born, seeds of greatness are placed within us from God.[3] God starts us all out with the necessary ingredients within us to succeed. Zig Ziglar says it this way in his book, **See You At The Top**. "Man was designed for accomplishment, engineered for success and endowed with the seeds of greatness." But it is what we do with these seeds that determine our outcome. He also says we are born to win. However, if the seeds are not nurtured properly; then, most likely,

> *The average person goes to his grave with the music still inside him.*

there will be a measure of deformity or delay. This does not, however, negate the plan of God for your life, but it certainly weighs on the process. We are solely responsible for how the seed is developed in our lives. Listen: It is said that the average person goes to his grave with the music still inside him.

Conflicts within are also obstructions to releasing greatness in our lives. When things are in harmony on the inside, we can make great connections with destiny on the outside. By becoming congruent on the inside, we can experience a connection on the outside where we enter into the flow of destiny that God intended for us.[4] In the cycle of life connections are constantly being made that pulls us toward our destiny and purpose in God. It is a series of ongoing prophetic encounters.

If you were to consider for a moment the chain of events that led you to the life you are living right now, you would see where all the dots are connected. And how one thing led to another and another until we arrive at the moment we call – "now." Some of us might not be happy with where we are now or better yet, we hear a voice within us calling and compelling us to go another place -- to take another path. Even though we might not have a clear understanding of this new way or new path, God will lead us by His Spirit into that which He has preordained for us. Remember, the Bible says the steps of a righteous man are ordered by the Lord (Psalm 37:23).

Have you ever felt compelled to do something that seemed somewhat asinine or just plain silly? Everything about these actions seems inconsequential. The Bible says God takes the foolish things of this world to confound the wise. It is times in our lives like this that this scripture rings

> *Divine connections are one of the core principles to us receiving our destiny...they are empowering agents.*

true. What we don't know in most of these uncertain instances is that divinity is still at work. God is divinely nudging and leading us to take a specific action because He will use this action as a spring board to get us to our next specific moment.

Divine connections

These actions are not some random chances of fate, but they are divine connections that God has arranged for our lives. It is God that causes us to connect with people that link us to our next stage in our destiny. Whether they unintentionally share something with us that might seem minute and mundane, the connection can be the very key to our next breakthrough.

Divine connections are one of the core principles to us receiving our destiny. It is the foundation of our life – an invisible web that connects us to God, ourselves, and others. And it is the vital principle for finding our unique path to success.[5] Divine connections are empowering agents. When we are connected divinely it empowers our journey as we move toward our unique path in God. As we connect with this uniqueness (our purpose and

> *We cannot divinely connect with something that is not divinely purposed for us.*

destiny); we become more aware of the sense of an inner certainty that will guide every major decision in our lives.

Divine moments and divine connections are gateways to our future. They are channels of blessings that ignite passion for the journey. If you lack passion in an area or a place you find yourself in; perhaps this is not the path God has ordained for you. As a matter of fact, the lack of motivation in an area is an indicator that something is not for you. We cannot divinely connect with something that is not divinely purposed for us.

Below are the indicators that Valorie Burton says in her book, **Listen**

To Your Life, shows whether you understand the principle of connection:

- You have a sense of divine purpose and destiny.
- You have a clear and compelling vision that keeps you persevering even in the face of failure and disappointment.
- You seek to learn the life lesson in every experience, even those that are difficult, negative, or tragic.
- You seek and experience spiritual growth on a continual basis.

Discovering Your Destiny

- You have defined success for yourself.
- Prayer is a part of your daily life and a way of strengthening your spiritual life.
- Your job, business and/or community involvement is an expression of your innermost values and desires.
- You spend some quiet time alone on a regular basis.
- You communicate openly, honestly, and effectively in your relationship with others.
- Because you fully

understand who you are and why you are here, you are confident about making major life decisions.
- Your financial plans and behavior reflect your vision and values.[6]

The Power of Vision

Connection places you on your unique path, but it is vision that energizes it and keeps you on course. When we can clearly see (internally) where God wants to take us; then the stages in the process will become empowered. A compelling vision is conceived with purpose and clothed with passion.[7] Any God-given vision will be birthed out of purpose. It is the fuel for the journey.

> *Men and women who have done great things for God have been people with great vision. They were individuals that saw what others could*

The more clearly or vividly that you can see the vision of God for your life, the more aggressive you will be in pursuing it. This is why vision is so important. It empowers your journey and energizes your thoughts. A compelling vision will guide you even though there are blind spots along the way.

Here are some attributes about vision:
- Vision doesn't just happen overnight – it is a process.
- Vision is easy to lose but hard to regain.
- Vision is absolutely necessary for survival.

- Visions must be written.
- Vision clarifies destination. Without it you are lost.
- Vision is God's way of getting you to think like Him – BIG
- Vision is within YOU – go find it.
- Vision never becomes a reality without action.
- True vision becomes a part of who we are.
- Where there is vision, there is provision.[8]

So the lack of vision or impaired vision is detrimental to your dream or destiny. Men and women who have done great things for God and in society have been people with great vision. They were individuals that saw what others could not see. We cannot go any further than where we can conceive. And we can never change our location until we determine our destination. The cloak of blindness must be removed off of our eyes if we are to achieve all that God wants us to accomplish.

The Power to Dream

I believe most of us have heard the song or cliché, "To Dream the Impossible Dream." But there is no such thing as an impossible dream with God. As a matter of fact, the Bible says all things are possible with God -- **"The things which are impossible with men are possible with God" (Luke 18:27).**

Many years ago I had the privilege of reading Dr. Robert Schuller's book on possibility. Dr. Schuller is a respected theologian and scholar among both, the religious and secular worlds. He is especially known for his glass cathedral church. Many call him the "possibility pastor." Reading his book has revolutionized my thinking and my life. I was transformed into a "possibility thinker."

The stage in my life in which I read this book was when I was really being challenged concerning my self-worth, my value and my contribution to the Christian community as a minister. It was a life saver for me. It encouraged me to keep dreaming because no matter what I was experiencing in the now, God still had my best interest and future in mind. So, no matter what you go through, God is not finished blessing you. The end of the matter is still out.

Men who dream great dreams sometimes become builders of great edifices.[25] It is dreamers that design large buildings. It was dreamers that wrote our Constitution. It was a dreamer that flew the first plane. Every great achievement is conceived first through a dream. Throughout the scriptures God used dreams many times to give men direction about their future, destiny and potential:

- King Abimelech – God showed King Abimelech in a dream that his life was coming to an end if he slept with Sarah, Abraham's wife. (Genesis 20:3)
- Joseph – God showed Joseph in a dream that he was going to be a ruler. (Genesis 37:5)
- The Butler and the Baker – God showed them in a

dream while in prison the events that were going to take place in their life in the near future.
(Genesis 40:5)
- Pharaoh – God showed Pharaoh in a dream the famine that was going to come upon the land and how he was to prepare for it. (Genesis 41:7)
- Nebuchadnezzar – God showed Nebuchadnezzar in a dream the destruction that was coming upon his life because of rebellion. (Daniel 2:3)
- Daniel – God showed Daniel in a dream things

and events that were going to come upon the earth. (Daniel 7)

- Joseph – God showed Joseph in a dream concerning Mary's pregnancy. (Matthew 1:20)
- The Wise Men – God showed the wise men in a dream that they were to go to a certain city. (Matthew 2:12)

We can never out dream God. In fact, being a dreamer is a part of God's prophetic mantle that will be released in the End Times. **"And it shall come to pass afterward, that I will pour out my spirit upon all flesh;**

and your sons and your daughters shall prophesy, your old men shall dream dreams, your young men shall see visions (Joel 2:28). So God is not afraid of us having dreams and aspirations. As long as your dream and aspiration line up with God's desire for your life, then keep on dreaming.

Many scoffed at Dr. Schuller's dream to build a crystal cathedral, but Dr. Schuller has the last laugh now. "Dreams are the substance of every great

> *The power to achieve is inside all of us. But it is what we do with this power that is the demarcation of whether we are successful or*

achievement" according to the late Dr. Edwin Cole, a nationally renowned men's advocate and motivational speaker. ***"Now faith is the substance of things hoped for, the evidence of things not seen" (Hebrews 11:1).***

The Power to Achieve

The difference between average people and achieving people is their perception of and response to failure according to John Maxwell, prolific author and leading authority on leadership and personal success. He believes that in order for an individual to endure opposition, there must be a sense of purpose. It is the fuel that empowers perseverance. How we view adversity and failure will determine the path we take in life. Whether we do great things in life or settle for status quo is often based on how we process adversity.

The power to achieve is inside all of us. But it is what we do with this power that is the demarcation of whether we are successful or not. Purpose is a success factor. This is why the need to discover our purpose is invaluable. When purpose is defined and pursued, success is inevitable. However, success is always a process. And it is the process, we often want to forfeit. Our road to success is usually comprised of numerous accounts of failures and mistakes.

This is why the process to purpose is not always palatable. I am reminded of an adage in John Maxwell's book, **"Failing Forward."** "We must give ourselves permission to fail and permission to excel." Here are some "Rules for Being Human" that was outlined in his book:

- Rule #1: You will learn lessons.
- Rule #2: There are no mistakes – only lessons.
- Rule #3: A lesson is repeated until it is learned.
- Rule #4: If you don't learn the easy lessons, they get harder.

- Rule#5: You'll know you've learned a lesson when your actions change.

Mistakes Are Not Permanent Markers

There is no escape! If you have lived on planet earth for a good deal of time; then you're going to make some mistakes. There's just no way around it. Mistakes are components of our life's journey. However, mistakes do not have to be permanent markers. Too often people have embraced mistakes as being a total failure in life. Mistakes are never the total picture; they are just channels that need adjustment as you pursue your destiny. In actuality, when mistakes are processed properly, they are stimulants that cajole us to change. People who are successful in life are able to view negative experiences as a part of the process. Our paths to achievement are often laced with chasm of failures. Never let momentary events become permanent markers.

> *We cannot achieve all that God has for us if we allow negativity to control our thoughts.*

We cannot achieve all that God has for us if we allow negativity to control our thoughts. Too many people have allowed negative situations in the past to color the way they view life today. Having a negative attitude and being overly pessimistic in life are sure ways of fostering failure. When dealing with mistakes, we must make the distinction as to whether they are a fact or truth. And more than likely, they are only a fact and not the truth. Having something being a fact doesn't necessarily make it a truth. Yes, we all make mistakes, but the truth of the matter is we are not defined by our mistakes. Just because you made a mistake in doing "some things," does not make you a failure in "all things." There is a difference.

Failure and Success is Defined Internally

Your definition of failure or success is an internal dialogue. It is an internal job. It is the final declaration or conclusion of the argument within that determines your present state of being. If you define failure as a self-worth issue; then your present state will be one of rejection and despondency. If you define failure as a learning tool; then your outlook on life will be positive. You will have a winning attitude.

> *The world looks at money, prestige, education, power, talent and recognition to determine one's worth and whether they are successful or not. God looks at purpose to validate our existence.*

Never attach failure to your self-worth or value. The worth of who you are should not be judged by your mistakes. The worth of who you are is determined by character, not mistakes. And most certainly, if you have a character flaw, please work on it. Giftings can only get you so far, but your character is the trait that will maintain your reputation and position.

The way the world defines success is different than the way God defines success. The world looks at money, prestige, education, power, talent and recognition to determine one's worth and whether they are successful or not. God looks at purpose to validate our existence. The more purpose driven we are in life, the more successful we will be in life. Our fixation should be on purpose and not popularity, prestige or power. In the words of one writer, "Great minds have purposes, others have wishes."

I like the way John Maxwell defines success:

Knowing your purpose in life
Growing to reach your potential
Sowing seeds that benefit others

The Path to Success

In February 2005, I was selected to receive an award for the "***BEST 2005 African-American Woman of the Year***" by a non-profit organization in the community, **Creative Visions Social Services.** Needless to say, this was quite an honor for me. But I was doubly blessed when they asked me also to be the keynote speaker for this wonderful ceremonial occasion.

My mother flew in from North Carolina to be with me in Dallas. I was showered with support by my family, several of my friends, co-laborers and colleagues in the ministry. It was truly a memorable event.

Weeks before the event, however, I found myself praying really hard asking God to give me the right thing to impart into the people's spirits that would be attending. It wasn't until the night before the event that I got clarity on what He wanted me to say. I knew whatever I said had to be community based as well as motivational. So as I prayed and pondered and pondered and prayed, God finally showed me what He wanted me to say.

The title of my speech was, **"It Takes A Village to Empower A City."** That night, I talked briefly about Hillary

Rodham Clinton's book, "**It Takes A Village,**" and how she challenged the village – grandparents, neighbors, teachers, policemen, ministers, employers, political leaders, community leaders, caregivers – to take responsibility in raising *all* children regardless of their biological parents.

Then God had me to share about another book I read by Dr. Marva Mitchell, "**It Takes A Church to Raise A Village.**" In Dr. Mitchell's book she raised the question whether the village today was adequately prepared to raise the children. Her conclusion: the village is sick. She said if the village is sick; then the village is no longer capable of raising the children when it is in need of being raised itself. How can the village be raised? How can the village be rescued? Who or what will it take to raise the village? Answer: The church.

Now, all across America the church has answered this call. Churches have gone into the community and offered numerous empowering and educational programs. They have built large activity centers to draw the youth and to give them alternatives to being in the streets. So, now the village is healing and streams of restitution are flowing from the village again. Therefore, the village now has the baton or responsibility again, but its sole responsibility is not only to raise the children, but to empower the city.

So, I spent about ten minutes sharing how the village can empower a city. And at the end of my speech God had me to outline four things that were critical to our personal paths of success. They were:

Be more solution conscious, than problem conscious – If we are going to achieve all that God has for us in this life, we must be more solution conscious, than problem conscious. It is always easier to point out the problem, but it takes a bigger person to see the solution.

Be a bridge, instead of a wall – A wall is an upright structure used to enclose or divide. A bridge is also a structure, but it is used to cross over on: It is a passage, gateway or gate. Both of these entities are structures, but one withholds and the other releases. One hinders and one supports. Let's be a bridge.

Be an advocate, instead of an adversary – Many people are known by what they are against. As people of destiny, we need to be recognized for what we are for and not what we are against. Because of my work in the community now, I am known as a Reconciliation Advocate or a Network Specialist. Both of these terms imply that I am against racism and bigotry. But I would rather be known as a Reconciliation Advocate than one who hates bigots. Do you see the difference?

Be someone who stirs up people's gifts and not one who stifles them – When we add value to people's lives, we, in actuality, are making the world a better place. We can never go wrong encouraging others and extending ourselves to be a bridge to help others get to the other side. People are always our best commodity to invest in. If you help enough people get what they want, you will become empowered to get everything you want in life. This is my life's mission and passion – to help others get what they want or be all they can be. If there is some way I can strengthen any area in someone's life; then I am going to do it. I don't need to ask a board, my pastor or friend. It is a natural response for me. Yes, I know sometimes people might take advantage of you, but I always retain the right or privilege when to stop supporting or giving to someone. There have been some instances that I had to do this, but I know I gave them my best when I was working with them. Purpose is about giving, not getting.

Failure is Not An Option

When you are striving to obtain the destiny of God for your life; then failure cannot be an option in your spirit. Therefore, opposition, setbacks and adversity must be responded to correctly. Failures can no longer be viewed as defeat. Never rewrite your philosophy in life to accommodate a tragedy. Tragedy is only a temporary setback. Dr. Phillip McGraw, Ph.D, national television talk show host, says, "Pain passes, principles are permanent." Now, this is the way the Bible expresses it: "...Weeping may endure for a night, but joy cometh in the morning" (Psalm 30:5b).

> *Depending on the record we play inside our head will determine how we see failure.*

There is a game show that comes on TV called "Friend or Foe." It is set up where each person has a partner they have to work with to get into the finals, but when they get there and upon taking their final challenge, they have to secretly choose whether the other person is a "Friend or Foe." If either of them chose "Foe," and the other one chooses friend, the one who chose foe would get all the money. But if they both chose "Foe," they both lose. However, if they both choose "Friend," they split whatever money they have accumulated throughout the game. Of course, the object here is to talk the other person into trusting you, so that as they choose "Friend" you wittingly choose "Foe" and ultimately take home all of the winnings.

Our failures in life can either be a friend or foe to us. Depending on the record we play inside our head will determine how we see failure. But if you are going to be a person who is striving for excellence, failure must become a friend and not a foe.

When you look at failure from this standpoint; then failure becomes a life lesson. Our bad experiences in life should be our classroom homework assignment. Like the old saying, "If you want something different out of life; then you have to do something different."

There are ten reasons people failed according to John Maxwell:

1. Poor People Skills
2. A Negative Attitude

3. A Bad Fit
4. Lack of Focus
5. A Weak Commitment
6. An Unwillingness to Change
7. A Shortcut Mind-Set
8. Relying on Talent Alone
9. A Response to Poor Information
10. No Goals

Let's view failure as a friend and not a foe.

Why Are We Here?

The greatest tragedy in life is not death, but life without a reason.[9] Feeling inadequate and/or insignificant are negative factors that have led many to suicide. We all want to feel special and cared

> *Purpose is more than just direction, but it is the very plumb line that our vision and destiny are assessed through and by.*

for and when there is a void in this area, it affects our vision. The search for significance is a travesty in our society. People have done many things to gain respect, power, prestige and recognition, but if there is a lack in this area, the end result is still the same -- void.

The search for significance must always start with the one who created us – God. In Mike Murdock's book, "Dream Seeds," he says, "Any reputable manufacturer is committed to the success of his product." When we were born, purpose was attached to our birth. So why were we born? We were born to fulfill the plan and purpose of God for our lives. I like the phrase that Dr. Myles Munroe, a nationally acclaimed minister of the gospel from the Bahamas, coined, "Wherever purpose is not known, abuse is inevitable."[10] If the lack of purpose is outstanding in a situation or circumstance; then any measure of movement or advancement could be faulty or even fatal.

Purpose is more than just direction, but it is the very plumb line that our vision and destiny are assessed through and by. Why are we doing this? Why are we going here? And why are we where we are? Purpose will answer all of these questions. The destiny of God is woven into the fabric and fiber of all of our souls. But if there is a lack of purpose, abnormality will exist. It is only when we fully understand the purpose and destiny of God for our lives that we can ever achieve or be all that God has for us. Our fulfillment in life is contingent upon recognizing and doing what we were born to be and do, for there is a prophetic word waiting to be fulfilled in all of our lives.

Dr. Shirley K. Clark

Chapter 2

Warfare is Inevitable

Dr. Shirley K. Clark

Being a Christian does not exempt us from trouble. And for some of us, when we received Christ into our lives were told that everything was going to be alright. However, this statement is an oxymoron as it relates to our Christian walk. Even though the Bible has promised that there will be a place of rest (Hebrews 4:9), there is still an inevitable measure of warfare that is associated with the life of a believer.

Reckoning with this truth; therefore, we have to posture ourselves for pending onslaughts from the evil one – Satan (II Timothy 3:12).

We Have an Enemy

In the book of Revelation, Chapter 13, verse 7 says that Satan has come to war with the saints and to overcome them. The book of Daniel says it this way; Satan has come to wear out the saints of the most High. Looking at these scriptures from the natural standpoint could possibly invoke fear. But when you "flip the coin" you will see that God has not left us without a promise.

Here is Apostle Paul's sentiment in II Corinthians 4:8, **"We are troubled on every side, yet not distressed; we are perplexed, but not in despair; persecuted, but not forsaken; cast down, but not destroyed."** God always has a "but" and a "yet" for His people. Though you might have trouble in your life, God's Word says you would not be in distress. Though you might be perplexed, you are not to be in despair. Persecuted, but you are never forsaken. Cast down, but not destroyed. This is a prophetic

> *Temptations are only opportunities for God to show His faithfulness*

scripture. There is a "but" and a "yet" in every situation we go through.

We are told also in the Word of God to count it all joy when we fall into divers temptations (James 1:2). Temptations are only opportunities for God to show His faithfulness – "There hath no temptation taken you but such as is common to man: but God is faithful, who will not suffer you to be tempted above that ye are able, but will with the temptation also make a way to escape, that ye may be able to bear it" (I Corinthians 10:13).

The Way of Escape

God will always provide us with a way of escape when going through trials and tribulations. But our way of escape is always attached to a prophetic word – "...but God is faithful." The faithfulness of God cannot be compared to the faithfulness of man. No matter how we feel we have captured the faithfulness of God in our finite mind, we still need to release God to do or move beyond our perception.

God's main concern in our lives is purpose. He is more concerned that His purpose be worked out in us and not our will. Ephesians 1:4-5 says, **"According as he hath CHOSEN US in** *him before the foundation of the world, that we should be holy and without blame before him in love. Having PREDESTINATED US unto the adoption of children by Jesus Christ to himself, according to the good pleasure of HIS WILL."*

The word "Predestinated" means to set boundaries before; limits.[11] It is not that God determined to do something when it was actually done, but that He intended to do it beforehand. We have a predetermined destiny in God. And it is your predetermined destiny that often elicits warfare in your life.

Your Destiny Determines Your Warfare

To win any type of war, there has to be an understanding of war.[12] We must know who, what, when, where, and most of all, why we are fighting. If God has singled an individual out for greatness, know that there will be an increase in spiritual warfare for this person. This is the way I define it -- little destiny, little warfare; big destiny, big warfare. If you are going through hell constantly in your life, know it is because God has a great destiny for you. God has greatness in your bowels. It has nothing to do with your nice clothes, hairstyle, pretty shoes, designer suits or luxury car. But it has everything to do with your destiny. Your destiny determines your warfare.

What is God calling you to do? If you are consistently receiving resistance in an area, it is because God has something great for you to do. The enemy wants to frustrate your purpose. When God instructed Nehemiah to rebuild the walls and the gates of Jerusalem, the first thing the enemy tried to do when they began

> *The devil will always try to hinder the move of God in our lives, and because some of us are pregnant with greatness, he wants us to*

to rebuild the walls was try and frustrate their purpose. "But it came to pass, that when Sanballat, and Tobiah, and the Arabians, and Ammonites, and the Ashdodites, heard that the walls of Jerusalem were made up, and that the breaches began to be stopped, then they were very wroth, and conspired all of them together to come and to fight against Jerusalem, and to hinder it." (Nehemiah 4:7-8).

The devil will always try to hinder the move of God in our lives, and because some of us are pregnant with greatness, he wants us to miscarry. If that doesn't work, then his next plan is to destroy us. When the devil could not stop the birth of Christ, then his next attack was to try and kill Him.

> *"When Herod the king had heard these things, he was troubled, and all Jerusalem with him...And when he had gathered all the chief priests and scribes of the people together, he demanded of them where Christ should be born.*
>
> *And being warned of God in a dream that they should not return to Herod...Arise, and take*

the young child and his mother, and flee into Egypt; and be thou there until I bring thee word: for Herod will seek the young child to destroy him.

Then Herod, when he saw that he was mocked...slew all the children that were in Bethlehem, and in all the coasts thereof, from two years old and under..."

Matthew 2:3-16

The devil was so incensed about the birth of Christ that every child two years old and under were killed. Now, I need you to really process this. If someone was to kill all the babies two years old and under right now in just your city alone what kind of effect do you think this would have on your city? I'll tell you what kind of effect it will have on your city. It would be a devastating monstrosity. Herod was being controlled so much by an evil spirit that he not only killed the babies in his local city, but he continued his lunatic rampage throughout the region. This is wickedness at its optimum level -- all of this to hinder the plan of God.

Because the devil will try to hinder the move of God in our life, we must be fortified and strategic like Nehemiah was in order to outwit him. Listen to what Nehemiah said, "Nevertheless we made our prayer *unto* our God, and set a watch against them day and night, because of them." You have to watch and pray. You must learn how to stay focused in the midst of opposition. You have to learn how to have a sword in one hand (a destroying weapon) and a brick in another (a building tool). Unless you acquire the skill of dexterity the devil will frustrate your purpose relentlessly.

Your Prophetic Word is a Weapon of Warfare

Your building tool is always your prophetic word. It is a weapon of warfare. Your prophetic word should predicate your actions. If you have prophetic words that have been spoken over your life; then it is these words that should be wielded at the devil to foil his tactics. This is called warring with your prophetic word. Apostle Paul tells Timothy in I Timothy 1:18, "This charge I commit unto thee son Timothy, according to the prophecies which went before on thee, that thou by them mightest war a good warfare."

When the enemy comes to frustrate your purpose, pull out your prophetic word or words and begin to declare them over your life. No matter what is going on, know that purpose is being worked out regardless.

Throughout the eons of time the prophets prophesied repeatedly that the Messiah was coming. They prophesied it and they prophesied it until eventually, the Bible said that the Word was made flesh and dwelt among us and we beheld His glory. You have to be relentless with your prophetic word until you see the manifestation of it. Your prophetic word is a weapon that will annihilate whatever the enemy is trying to conjure up or do in your life. God wants to bring flesh to your prophetic word.

Because the prophets remained consistent in proclaiming that there was a coming savior, they caused an atmosphere throughout history for the prophetic word to be germinated within. As each prophet's life came to an end, the prophetic word; however, continued to echo within the hearts and spirits of the prophets who were yet living. Each generation of prophets kept or was responsible for the prophetic word moving in the direction toward its manifestation. It was their prophetic proclamations that facilitated the manifestation of God's purpose being fulfilled.

> *"And his father Zacharias was filled with the Holy Ghost, and prophesied saying, Blessed be the Lord God of Israel; for he hath visited and redeemed his people,*
>
> *And hath raised up an horn of salvation for us in the house of his servant David; as he spake **by the***

mouth of his holy prophets, which have been since the world began."

Luke 1:67-70

Chapter 3

Prospering in the Midst of Opposition

Dr. Shirley K. Clark

F or the most part, I believe most people know the story in the book of Exodus about the children of Israel, and how they were in slavery for 400 years under the rule of Pharaoh.

But most people, however, might not realize that before the children of Israel's captivity their lives were completely different. And before their exile into captivity, the children of Israel

> *When you are successful, all types of spirits will be lurking around to deceive, distract and discourage you to get you out of the will of God for your life.*

were very prosperous people. Their lives were a depiction of splendor and prosperity. It was a mirror of God's goodness as well as His faithfulness. "And the children of Israel were fruitful, and increased abundantly, and multiplied, and waxed exceedingly mighty." (Exodus 1:7)

However, their situation changed abruptly. It says in Exodus, chapter one, verse eight, a new king arose (a new move, a new supervisor, another transition, another warfare) that disrupted the lifestyle of the children of Israel.

I submit to every believer that when everything is going well in your life, this is the most critical and dangerous stage in your walk with God. Why? Because success has a way of blinding you. When you are successful, all types of spirits will be lurking around to deceive, distract and discourage you (pride, selfishness, prayerlessness, etc.) to get you out of the will of God for your life.

As God's people (children of Israel) became so engrossed with their success, they lost sight of the enemy approaching. Sometimes, as God begins to move people toward their destiny, they become preoccupied with their immediate successes instead of continuing to focus on the end product. When this happens, their destiny is delayed. I Peter 5:8 tells us that we are to "Be sober, be vigilant; because your adversary the devil, as a roaring lion walketh about, seeking whom he may devour." We must be watchful and sober at all times. Our little successes along the way, while we should celebrate them, are not the ultimate prize or goal we should be settling for. Destiny is what we should be after.

> *Sometimes as believers the reason we cannot go any further in God is because we are still holding onto old ways and misguided mindsets of the past.*

When the children of Israel were taken into captivity, continually and daily their taskmasters afflicted them with heavy burdens, but the good news is the more they afflicted them, the more they multiplied and grew (see Ex. 1:11-12). **God wants us to prosper in the midst of opposition!**

Encountering Opposition

When opposition arises, there are six things we must know that are essential to outwitting the devil according to Dr. Millicent Thompson in her book, **Don't Die in the Winter.**

1. We must understand what opposition is.
2. We must ask the Lord to help us remain positive.
3. We must take a stand against the enemy.
4. We must do what God tells us to do.
5. We must pray for our enemies.
6. We must seek God in faith.[13]

All of these things are critical, if we are to grow and multiply during adversity (warfare). Also, when we are going through trials and tribulations, God might require that we get rid of some things. There are some things He wants us to deal with and there are some things we might have to lay aside.

Conquering the Strongholds in Your Life

Like David in I Samuel 6:15-17, he had five giants in his life that he had to conquer — **The city of Ashdod; the city of Gaza; the city of Ashkelon; the city of Gath; and the city of Ekron**

— in order to continue to walk in victory and pursue the destiny of God for his life.

The city of Ashdod was the first city David had to defeat. This city was located on a hill (a high and lofty place), which is symbolic of pride.[14] When pride is present in a believer's life, it is a tremendous roadblock to reaching one's destiny in God. Pride will always give you a distorted view of things. It is like being in an airplane in the sky, everything below looks distorted. This is exactly what pride will do in you. It will cause you to be self-absorbed, which will open the door for a critical spirit to come upon your life. However, if we expect to see continuous breakthroughs in our lives, then one must destroy the spirit of Pride. The Bible says pride goes before a fall (see Proverbs. 16:18). It is the little foxes that spoil the vine (Song of Solomon 2:15).

The second city David had to conquer was Gaza. Gaza means stronghold. A stronghold is a fortified place; a fortress. It is said that 95% of all strongholds originate in the mind. Sometimes, as believers, the reason we cannot go any further in God is because we are still holding onto old ways and misguided mindsets of the past. The Bible says we cannot put new wine in old wine skin. Thoughts, imaginations, reasonings, and speculations that are contrary to the Word of God, must be pulled down in the spirit. II Corinthians 10:4-5 say, "For the weapons of our warfare are not carnal, but mighty through God to the pulling down of strongholds; Casting down imaginations, and every high thing that exalteth itself against the knowledge of God and bringing into captivity every thought to the obedience of Christ."

> *Affliction, persecution, difficulties, and problems should be looked at as opportunities for your life to be refined.*

In James Allen's book, ***As A Man Thinketh,*** he says, "A man's mind may be likened to a garden, which may be intelligently cultivated or allowed to run wild; but whether cultivated or neglected, it must, and will, bring forth."[15] He also says, "Until thought is linked with purpose there is no intelligent accomplishment.[16] The strongest and dominate thoughts that satiate our minds will be the direction we will be guided toward. That which controls us is that which masters our thoughts. It is absolutely essential that you dismantle erroneous thoughts and misconceptions that are plaguing your mind. If not, your destiny will be thwarted. Your destiny will be aborted or an illegitimate destiny will come forth.

The third city David had to defeat in order to continue to flow in the purpose of God for his life was Ashkelon. This city was one of the finest principal and prosperous cities of the Philistines. What does this city represents — greed, prosperity, and selfishness.[17] When God begins to bless you, you must remember to always give God the glory. It is God that gives you power to get wealth (Duet. 8:18). So if you forget God as He promotes you, you will invite destruction upon your life. When

God prospers you, you are obligated to give Him the glory.

The next city David had to conquer was the city of Gath. Gath means wine press.[18] Just like wine has to be refined for the best to come out of it, you have to go through some things for the best to come out of you. Remember in St. John 15, it says that every branch that beareth fruit, he purgeth that it might bring forth more fruit.

Maturity takes time. Fruit does not develop overnight, but over a period of time. The tree that bears the fruit must have the right amount of water, must be planted in the right kind of soil, and must have the right temperature. Affliction, persecution, difficulties, and problems should be looked at as opportunities for your life to be refined. Remember: wine is better when aged.

The last giant David had to conquer was the city of Ekron. Ekron means barrenness, torn apart, extermination. Baalzebub was the god of Ekron (Lord of flies).[19] Have you ever had a fly buzzing around you? If so, you found it hard to keep your focus while this was going on. Distraction is one of Satan's greatest weapons against saints when in warfare. If he can get you to lose your focus in warfare, your victory is uncertain. The word "distraction"

> *Getting to your "Promised Land" will be met with opposition. And dealing with opposition properly will secure your future.*

literally means "to drag around in a circle."[20] This is what Satan wants the believer to do — drag around in a circle — no fruit being born and no victory being won. In other words, we are barren and unfruitful.

However, if we are going to prosper in the midst of opposition, you have to pull down the strongholds that are in your life. You have to search your heart and make sure that the enemy does not have anything inside of you (see John 14:30). God wants to prosper you, but you must do some things first. You must get rid of excess baggage, lay aside every weight that easily besets you, and walk in the spirit and not in the flesh.

Driving Out the "Ites"

With the Red Sea experience behind them and the hope of a "Promise Land" before them, the children of Israel sighed, thinking of the rest that awaited them. But the moment of truth came when God revealed to the children of Israel, yes, I do have a promised land for you, but you will still have to fight to attain it.

> *"When the Lord your God brings you into the land which you go to possess, and has cast out many nations before you, the Hittites and the Girgashites and the Amorites and Canaanites and Perizzites and Hivites and the Jebusites, seven nations great and mighter than you, and when the Lord your God delivers them over to you, **you shall conquer them and utterly***

***destroy them.** You shall make no covenant with them nor show mercy to them."*

Deuteronomy 7:1-2

Getting to your "Promised Land" will be met with opposition also. And dealing with opposition properly will secure your future. I liked what God told the children of Israel. He not only required them to conquer their enemies, but their ultimate assignment was to utterly destroy them. This is what we have to do in the spirit when opposition comes to obstruct the destiny of God in our lives as well. We have to kill it and it has to be done at the root. We cannot war from a symptom mentality, but from an origin mentality. What is the thing that is giving life to this obstruction? What is the source? When we deal with the root, we isolate and annihilate the source of the problem.

God told the children of Israel, that all of the strongholds that would arise to impede their destiny, He would deliver into their hand, however, He was leaving it up to the children of Israel, to destroy them.

The Hitties: The first nation that God listed that He had given them was the Hitties. The Hitties were known for their combatant military strength and superiority. And because of this, nations, regions, and people were severely threatened by them. Their name means *"one who is feared"*.[21] It is said that the Hitties were the most feared nation in the ancient world. So, literally, all the Hitties had to do was threaten war with nations and surrounding regions and they would retreat. They would run and hide.

Sometimes the threat of something happening is more terrifying and tormenting than the actual event itself. Just hearing about a pending danger or horrific weather condition can make one's heart begin to flutter and elevate our adrenaline. Anxiety and fear can grip your soul so bad that it will cause you to be immobilized.

There is no better story in the Bible that depicts this better than the story of David and Goliath. It is an excellent example of this. An entire army of strong and trained warriors were paralyzed by the threat of one man -- Goliath. The scripture records it this way:

> *"And the Philistines stood on a mountain on the side, and Israel stood on a*

mountain on the other side: and there was a valley between them.

And there went out a champion out of the camp of the Philistines, named Goliath, of Gath, whose height was six cubits and a span.

And he had an helmet of brass upon his head, and he was armed with a coat of mail; and the weight of the coat was five thousand shekels of brass.

And he had greaves of brass upon his legs, and a target of brass between his shoulders.

And the staff of his spear was like a weaver's beam; and his spear's head weighed six hundred shekels of iron: and one bearing a shield went before him.

And he stood and cried unto the armies of Israel, and said unto them, *Why are ye come out to set your battle in array? am* *not I a Philistine, and ye servants to Saul? choose you a man for you, and let him come down to me.*

If he be able to fight with me, and to kill me, then will we be your servants: but if I prevail against him, and kill him, then shall ye be our servants, and serve us.

And the Philistine said, I defy the armies of Israel this day; give me a man, that we may fight together.
I Samuel 17:3-10

Now, listen to what the scripture says that Saul and the army of Israel did:

> *"When Saul and all Israel **heard** those words of the Philistine, they were dismayed, and greatly afraid."*
>
> *I Samuel 17:11*

Just the threats of Goliath made Israel to retreat. They were greatly afraid. Fear overtook them so much that

> *When you become double minded, you cannot make sound decisions.*

not a man would confront and advance toward the enemy. If we do not conquer the spirit of the Hittite in our lives, we will be rendered helpless in times of opposition. And it most certainly will hinder you from reaching your purpose and destiny in God. The Bible says God has not given us the spirit of fear, but power, love and sound mind (2 Timothy 1:7).

If you let fear reign, it will "split" your mind. In other words, you become double minded. The Bible says a double minded man is unstable in all its way (James 1:8). When you become double minded, you cannot make sound decisions. Therefore, you will not prosper in the kingdom of God. It takes a sound mind to make sound decisions ---...but he has given us...a sound mind.

A sound mind is a stable mind. A sound mind is a "whole" mind. It is a whole mind that is able to discern between good and evil. What is the devil threatening you with right now in your life? Perhaps, he is holding you in captivity because of past sins. Perhaps, he is telling you, you will never mount up to anything. Perhaps, he is telling you that God does not love you. If this is you, don't believe the lie. Come against these tormenting spirits that are bombarding your mind and render them powerless to the power of God that rests upon your life -- God has given you power.

The Girgashites: The next spirit God wanted the children of Israel to destroy in their lives was the spirit of the Girgashites. This spirit is a self-destructive spirit. It means "dwellers of clay soil; fat and overweight."[22] This is the spirit that will cause one to be lethargic, sluggish

> *If we want to be continually used by God and to birth out God's dream for our lives; then we must stay humble.*

and unconcerned. It weighs on you physically and its function is to make you feel overwhelmed and depressed.

The Girgashites spirit is a silent killer because if you give into this spirit, it will not only cause you to feel depressed, but it could lead you to suicide. Each level of the enemy's tactics that you give into opens the door for him to attack you with the next level or might I say a higher level of torment to harass your mind. Like the old adage says, "Give someone an inch and they will take a mile."

God has designed your life to be used for His purpose. The Girgashite spirit wants to rob you of the very thing that God has designed for your life.[23]

The Amorites: The Amorites was another nation that the children of Israel were to conquer and destroy. The Amorites people were known for their prestigious clout and lofty positions. They had a high societal spirit upon them. They were a prideful nation that looked down on others. They were known for their intrusive manner and aggressive decorum.[24]

> *We were created with and for purpose. We were not an accident.*

The Bible says pride goes before a fall (Proverbs 16:18). It also says it bringeth shame (Proverbs 11:2). God cannot use us when we are prideful. After all, this is the spirit that got Satan kicked out of heaven (Isaiah 14:12-14). God looks for humble people to use in His kingdom. God looks for people He can trust. If we want to be *continually* used by God and to birth out God's dream for our lives; then we must stay humble.

The Canaanites: The Canaanite spirit is an unruly and disorder spirit.[25] It reaps havoc wherever it goes. Its main purpose is to "divide and conquer." We will run into these spirits that are represented in Canaan's offspring in our daily walk with the Lord as we try to enter and possess the land.[26] I have lived long enough to know that these spirits will be lurking in almost every environment or situation we will encounter. You have to be adamant and watchful to keep from falling prey to Canaanite spirits.

What this spirit wants to do is keep your mind in disarray and confused, so that you will have a lack of focus. This disorder spirit produces a condition so that our souls and minds are in captivity to the situations and circumstances in life.

We must not let this Canaanite spirit prevail in our lives. God is a God of order and when we align ourselves with His order of government (structure), we will be enabled to live a victorious life.

The Perizzites: The Perizzite nation had to be destroyed as well. This nation represents insecurity. The Perizzite spirit makes you feel unprotected. Perizzite means "dwelling in unwalled villages" or "village without walls."[27]

Insecure people are people that feel their lives have no meaning: It lacks purpose. But if you are in the family of God, nothing can be further than the truth than this. We were created with and for purpose. We were not an accident. We were designedly crafted and accepted in the beloved (Ephesians 1:6). You are somebody. Greater is He that is in you than He that is in the world (I John 4:4).

Furthermore, we are not alone. We are not by ourselves. We are not without protection. The Bible says the angel of the Lord encamps around those that fear the Lord. "The angel of the Lord encampeth round about them that fear him, and delivereth them" (Psalm 34:7). We are well protected in God (See Psalm 46).

Discovering Your Destiny

The Hivites: The Hivite spirit is characterized as being a spirit that keeps you from the fresh oil of God or keeps you from receiving the freshness of God.[28] This Hivite spirit is a descendant of the disorder spirit – the Canaanite spirit. The Hivite spirit is also said to be

> *What we won't acknowledge, we can't deal with.*

a wicked spirit.[29] Isn't it just like the devil to try and keep God's people from receiving from God daily -- Give us this day our daily bread?

I don't know about you, but I want a fresh move of God in my life every day. I don't want yesterday's stale bread; I want today's fresh anointing. But it is this Hivite evil spirit that will invade our lives and cause us to settle for second best. Having a *consistent* prayer life will conquer the Hivite spirit in our lives. This spirit cannot survive or reside where the glory of the Lord is constantly abiding.

The Jebusites: The Jebusites are also a descendant of Canaan. Jebusite means to pollute, to trample down and to kick out.[30] This is what the devil wants to do in our lives. He wants to contaminate our lives with negative influences, so that he can walk all over us and utterly destroy us. The Jebusite spirit is a major stronghold. Out of all of the nations that God instructed Israel to conquer and destroy, they could not defeat the Jebusites. Scripture records it this way:

> "As for the Jebusites the inhabitants of Jerusalem, the children of Judah could not drive them out: but the Jebusites dwell with the children of Judah at Jerusalem unto this day.
> Joshua 5:63

However, God did not forget His promise and many years later God raised up David who overthrew and conquered the city of the Jebusites. We must not let any of these spirits reside in our lives because all of these spirits are hindrances to us receiving the promises of God for our lives. And no matter how innocent something might look, but if it resembles these types of spirits we need to ward them off and reject them. As long as the Jebusites were in the land, David could not fully come into his destiny.[31] It was after he had destroyed this stronghold that he was able to enter into his full kingdomship.

If we would do a trace throughout the Canaanite's lineage or family tree, we would see as each generation was birthed, they grew and became stronger and stronger. And because the Canaanite spirit was not dealt with properly from the beginning, it became a major stronghold in the children of Israel's lives. Look at the progression:

First, it started out just being a disorder spirit -- a spirit that represents confusion. Next, it was the Hivites – the spirit that keeps you from moving in the new things in God; the fresh oil of God. Finally, the Jebusite spirit – the spirit that comes to pollute your mind and life about the things of

God, so that you may be utterly destroyed will take root.

You see, you have to deal with things when they arise at the very beginning. What we won't acknowledge, we can't deal with. And what we won't deal with will ultimately destroy us. If you are going to be a great leader in the kingdom of God; then you must have tenacity and boldness. Great Leaders know how to handle opposition.

I like what J. Konrad Hole' says in his book, **The Making of a Cutting Edge Leader**. He says there are seven things every potential great leader must understand and assess properly: Accusation, Achieving, Adversity, Assignment, Associations, Attitude and Belief Systems. Here are some of the things he says under each category.

ACCUSATION: Never spend more time defending yourself to an enemy, than you do multiplying yourself in a protégé.

- Accusation is your enemies' way of influencing your future, by intimidating your present.
- Your response to accusation, determines how far off course your enemy can detour you.

- Accusation can only go as far as fact.
- No one will ever be influenced against you that have interrogated what they've heard, more than listened to what they've heard.
- Success is just a reward, for not defending yourself to wrong people.

ACHIEVING: Never spend more time mastering the "Art of Desire," more than you do the "Art of Possessing."

- Achievers are married to their goal, not their plan
- Achievers never consult another's' approval for identity.
- Achievers never consult those stuck in "Yesterday," about ideas for "Tomorrow."
- Achievers only pursue information, from those ahead of them.

ADVERSITY: Adversity is what your enemy uses for a crisis, and God uses for a classroom.

- Adversity is not an enemy, it's just the proof you have one.

- Adversity is the prelude to promotion.
- Adversity is an indicator of the worth of your goals.
- Adversity will only be as merciful as others that you have covered in their adversity.

ASSIGNMENT: Never defend your future to anyone who is not assigned to be a part of it.

- Your assignment is the solution somebody has been praying for.
- Your assignment is proof that God preserved you in

order to preserve His purpose in you.

- Your assignment will either be promoted or distracted by a person.
- Your assignment will attract sabotage the moment you are outside of it.
- Your assignment will only flourish in the place God leads you to.
- Your assignment was created an original, don't make it a copy.
- Your assignment will at times require you to move without the support of others.

ASSOCIATIONS: Never associate with anything you are unwilling to defend.

- You will never be bigger than the associations you keep.
- Every person you become connected to has other associations in their life, just like themselves.
- You will be known as much for the people you avoid as the ones that you associate with.
- The associations you permit will yield the results you have to live with.

- Your associations will help you or hurt you according to the boundaries you set for them.
- Never allow you associations to be lead by those with lesser character than you.

ATTITUDE: Never believe being successful is greater than being respected.

- Project the attitude that will reflect what you want other people to believe about you.
- Your approach to anything determines your success or failure in it.

- Somebody somewhere is always watching how you handle yourself.
- Your attitude will only be as "hopeless" as your near sighted focus or as "hopeful" as your farsighted vision.

BELIEF SYSTEM: Never protect a belief system that has not produced a victory.

- Those that speak into your life determine what you believe about it.
- A person's belief system is what determines a person's integrity system.

Discovering Your Destiny

- Your future will only be as big as your ability to restructure your methodology.
- You will never change your belief system until something you have a belief in cannot produce something you have a desire for.[32]

Dr. Shirley K. Clark

Chapter 4
What to do When You Get A Prophetic Word

This chapter is designed to teach you about some of the practical tips on what to do when you get a prophetic word. So many believers are confused about what to do or how to respond to a prophetic word. Prophetic words are sacred words from the throne of God, and they must be handled and governed properly. God has used the medium of "prophecy" throughout church history to be the forerunner of every major advent. So, this chapter is set aside to give you guidelines on how to handle personal prophecy in your life. This teaching is not an inclusive argument, but rather, it is a foundational base to you receiving and activating prophetic words that are spoken over your life.

However, it is critical from the onset to place personal prophecy in its proper perspective. The theological and practical significance of the Pauline epistles rest somewhat in their tendency to place principles, concepts and practices in proper relationship to one another. Spiritual ministry, according to Paul, should be descent, orderly, judged by eldership, and a source of edification for the whole church (1 Corinthians 12-14). It was Paul who listed prophecy along with revelation, knowledge and doctrine as being necessary ingredients for the profiting of the saints (1 Corinthians 14:6).

Perhaps, Paul's reference to prophecy may have included the writings of the Old Testament prophets in addition to his personal ministry to the saints. Nevertheless, such a list places prophecy in a relationship with sound Biblical teaching and instruction. It also implies the responsibility of the believer to use common sense and sound judgment in making decisions affecting the issues of life. Scriptural prophecy is inspired speech that communicates divine purposes and intentions. It is profitable for encouragement, exhortation, comfort, reproof, rebuke, doctrine and instruction in righteousness.[37]

There are four things we need to do when we receive personal prophecy:

1. Transcribe Your Prophetic Word:

When you receive a prophetic word from the Lord, you need to transcribe it. You cannot war with a word you do not know. Habakkuk 2:2 says write the vision and make it plain.

Discovering Your Destiny

When you receive a prophetic word from the Lord, you are going to need to slow your "jump and shout" down long enough to hear what God is saying.

This is why I like the presbytery -- where mature gifts in the body of Christ are stationed at the altar with cassette recorders to capture the prophetic words as they are spoken to the people. When they finish prophesying, they hand the cassette tape to the recipients. The people have immediate access to the word that was spoken over his or her life.

If God is taking the time to speak a word into your life, then it is vitally important for you to hear and comprehend it. The word of God was written by men, but inspired by God (II Timothy 3:16). Prophetic words that come from the mouths of true anointed men and women of God are equally important. They are inspired words and utterance from God and they should be treated with reverence – "For the prophecy came not in old time by the will of man: but holy men of God spake as they were moved by the Holy Ghost" (II Peter 1:21). Therefore, you need to hear what God is saying.

With the exception of about two prophecies, I have all of my prophecies written down. Nationally renowned Evangelist Mike

Murdock said if you write a goal down in the natural it increases the chances of it coming to pass by ninety percent. How much more will a *prophetic* word come to pass that is spoken out of the mouth of a *prophetic* vessel inspired by a *prophetic* God? Increase, increase is all I see.

When I was working in the marketplace and a year before I left my job, I was introduced to how to write out a mission statement and how to write out my goals and visions for my life. Not only was I taught how to write them, but also how to outline what positive changes would be achieved in my life if I received each goal and vision. I had to put together a timeline of how I wanted each thing to happen and what tools or resources I might possibly need to help me acquire them. This process took a little while because it challenged me to inventory my life, organize my thoughts, and to judge my motives. In less than one year three-fourth of my requests were met.

One of the things I put on my list was to be a full time housewife. At the time I wrote my mission statement, I was barely making over twenty thousand a year and my husband was making probably double this amount. Everything we made went mostly to take care of bills. We were buying a home, but between the mortgage, childcare, home repairs, and utility bills, we lived from paycheck to paycheck.

One day my husband received a call from a corporate executive from MCI wanting to talk with him about a technical translations position. I believe someone he once worked with submitted his name to this person. The day he received the call, he was excited, but as they talked more, he realized it required relocation. So he wasn't as thrilled. We were living in North Carolina at this time and there were two locations available: Virginia and Dallas.

I have always felt in my spirit that I was going to live in Dallas, so I was very excited about the opportunity. However, my husband declined to take the job. But the corporate executive continued to pursue him. This executive wanted him so bad that this process went on for about three to four months. One time my husband said yes; then he changed his mind and said no. Finally, the executive called and asked what would it take to persuade him to accept the job. My husband negotiated a tremendous salary increase and he asked for several incentives; which included a complete relocation package.

Within months we moved to Dallas, TX and I became a housewife. When we estimated the amount of money we were paying for childcare, lunch and gas, it became feasible for me to stay at home.

My husband did not go out looking for this opportunity, but I believe God honored my written request. Since then, God used this job to be a launching pad to thrust my husband's salary into the six figures range. When you operate out of or do things based on a prophetic word, the totality of a matter is never fully revealed until the end. You never know what God wants to do in your life in its fullness.

But if you would get some order into your life, God would do the same for you – write the vision and make it plain. From my original mission statement there are only one or two things that have not come to pass yet, but regardless, I know they are coming.

Prophecy Has No Expiration Date

There is no expiration date assigned to a prophecy in the natural. However, prophecy can be delayed if your life is not in accordance to the Will of God. If you want the purpose and destiny of God to be worked out in your life, then you must walk godly. The condition for the blessings of God to continue to flow in the children of Israel's lives in Deuteronomy, Chapter 28 was that they had to hearken diligently to the voice of the Lord and walk in His statutes. You cannot do what you want to do if you want the blessings of God to overtake your life. You must be holy!

It's God's Timing

Prophecies will come to pass in God's timing and not your timing. I am seeing God fulfill some prophecies now that were prophesized to me over twenty years ago. God is the only one that knows when it is time to bring a word to pass. Jeremiah 29:11 says, "I know the thoughts I have for you, thoughts of good and not evil and to give you an expected end. God has an expected end for you."

In order for someone to grasp the full understanding of the timing of the Lord, he or she must understand biblical prophetic terminology of time. God's terminology of time differs considerably from ours. Because of this dichotomy, there have been great failures and frustration in the lives of many. The spirit of impatience often gets the best of most people. We must not get ahead of God.

In Dr. Bill Hamon's book, **Prophets & Personal Prophecy**, he offers this insight on the terminology of the timing of God:

> **Immediately** means from one day to three years.
>
> **Very soon** means one to ten years.

Now or **this day** means one to forty years.

I will without a definite time designation means God will act sometime in the person's life if he is obedient.

Soon was the term Jesus used to describe the time of His soon return almost two thousand years ago. "Behold, I come quickly."[38]

When we consider these terminologies, there is an indication that all prophecies are conditional or involve a process. For example: King Naaman was told in 2 Kings, Chapter 5 that God was going to heal his leprosy, but he had to dip seven times in the muddy waters of Jordan before the prophecy would come to pass. This was a conditional prophecy. And because it was conditional, Naaman almost missed his blessing because of the spirit of pride. He thought because he was a king, God should have instructed him to dip in the clear bodies of water within his region. Pride is always a barrier to the blessings of God. However, because King Naaman obeyed the prophecy from the prophet of God, he was healed.

2. Guard Your Prophetic Word:

Sometimes as Christians we talk too much. Some prophetic words you receive you cannot tell some people. Some things you need to keep to yourself. When the angel of the Lord appeared unto Mary and spoke a prophetic word into her life, it says she kept all things and pondered them in her heart.

Joseph, in the book of Genesis, got in trouble for talking too much. When God shared with Joseph what

He wanted to do in his life, Joseph shared it with his brothers and they became enraged. They became so incensed that they sold him into slavery.

Dream Killers

It is said that people are negative by nature. And it takes a tremendous amount of energy to break this cycle. This is why everybody is not able to handle what God wants to do in their life. Sometimes your vision can

The devil will always have dream killers to demise or ridicule what God is doing in your life.

be so big until other people can't possibly comprehend that God wants to do this for you. Plus, not everybody is happy with what God is doing or wants to do for you. This was so true in Joseph's situation in Genesis, Chapter 37. These types of people are individuals that I call dream killers. The devil will always have dream killers to demise or ridicule what God is doing in your life. Listen to what Joseph's brothers said when they saw him coming toward them – "And they said one to another, Behold, **this dreamer cometh**" (Genesis 37:19). Can't you hear the disdain in this statement?

Dreamers are possibility thinkers and dream killers are impossibility thinkers. You see the difference in a dreamer and a dream killer is that a dreamer sees their dream as a reality in their spirit way before it is ever manifested in the natural. And a dream killer can never see beyond its own negative experiences and unfulfilled desires. This is why it is hard to persuade a dreamer to forget about a dream when his mind is made up. You see, a God-given dream is hard to shake off because images of the dream are constantly being played repeatedly inside their spirit and mind.

So, no matter what happened to Joseph in the interim to his destiny, he used his dream as the compass for staying on course. No matter what his family thought about him. No matter what Potiphar's wife said about him. Joseph's success was based on his identification with God and not how others defined him. Thirteen years Joseph encountered repeated negative experiences, but he never lost faith in God's goodness. And because he didn't, he prospered. Remember: Nobody on earth can make you feel inferior without your permission. God's purpose will always take everything that you have ever gone through or going through to develop your full potential. This is why Joseph could declare at the end of the matter, "But as for you, ye thought evil against me: but God meant it unto good..." (Genesis 50:20).

> *When someone's dreams have been shattered, this can be a dangerous state for him or her because a wounded spirit will lead to all sorts of bad behaviors.*

Shattered Dreams

Occasionally, I will run into people who are hurting so much internally that they can no longer dream. Their hope factor is non-existent.

Their dreams and aspirations in life had been sorely destroyed. It is not that they wanted to be in this state. It was just that so many negative experiences happened so fast in their life that they didn't have adequate amount of time to properly process them. Therefore, they have a lack of trust for others and when you reach out to help them, they often withdraw.

When someone's dreams have been shattered, this can be a dangerous state for him or her because a wounded spirit will lead to all sorts of bad behaviors. "The spirit of a man will sustain his infirmity; but a wounded spirit who can bear?"

(Proverbs 18:14). Sometimes a wounded spirit will lead one to alcohol and drug abuse. Other times it can lead to suicide. However, there is always hope in God. No matter what you have endured, if you will keep believing for change, it will come. Even in your distraught state, your life still has potential and God wants to birth greatness out of you. It takes courage, but you can do it. Greater is He (God) that is in you than he that is in the world (I John 4:4). It is said heroes are individuals to whom courage has become visible.

You must believe against hope. The Bible says hope maketh not ashamed (Romans 5:5). If you can hope again, you can live again. One writer wrote, "We are not to live a crucified life, but a resurrected life." But no other story in the Bible portrays someone who lived out of a resurrected mentality than Job. He didn't give up on God when everything went bad in his life. In one day, Job lost everything. He lost family. He lost his livestock. He lost his income. He lost his health. No doubt Job had to deal with a lot of mental anguish, but he chose to have hope in the midst of the storm. How we handle pressure often determines whether we will succeed or fail. Job handled it correctly and in the end he received double for his trouble.

> "And the Lord turned the captivity of Job, when he prayed for his friends: also the Lord gave Job twice as much as he had before...so the Lord blessed the latter end of Job more than his beginning for he had fourteen thousand sheep, and six thousand camels, and a thousand yoke of oxen, and a thousand she asses. He had also seven sons and three daughters...And in all the land were no women found so fair as the daughters of Job: and

their father gave them inheritance among their brethren...So Job died, being old and full of days."

Job 42:10-17

Your Dream, Your Leader's Dream

Also, sometimes when greatness is upon your life, your leader might not be able to comprehend it. Sometimes God will require that you not share it with them *for a season*. Because leaders sometimes have expectations for you as a member, it is often hard for them to embrace God steering you in another direction.

This does not make them bad people, it just makes them human. If you are a parent, you should understand this. You know sometimes your children choose other paths of careers, ministries, education, marriage, etc. that might not meet your expectations. If you were honest, when this happened, this was a real frustration for you. I know, because I went through a situation like this with my daughter.

Thank God, My Daughter is Taking Violin Lessons

I am not sure when I acquired a liking for the violin, but I was elated when I learned about all the opportunities that were available for a skilled violinist. So when my daughter started taking violin lessons when she was around eight years old I envisioned all the engagements and opportunities that she was going to have as a professional violinist. But after about two years of private lessons, my daughter no longer wanted to continue with the violin. Needless to say, I was sorely disappointed.

I tried to explain to her about all the opportunities a professional violinist would have and how rare violinists are, especially African-Americans. I took great interest in her practice assignments. I took her to all her lessons. I made sure she watched violinists' performances on television. I did everything I could to maintain her interest, but to my dismay she was not happy playing the violin. She was very gifted with the violin and played very well, but it wasn't in her heart. I finally came to terms within myself that this was my dream and not hers.

> *There is an incubation period and a development stage for every prophetic word.*

When my daughter entered middle school she chose to play the flute. From day one till now she has enjoyed the flute immensely. By the end of her first school year, she was playing two grade levels above. I never had to push or encourage her to practice. She was self-motivated. She set up a schedule to practice after school every day. Plus, she was so gifted that she was offered a scholarship to take private flute lessons. This was what God had for her and not what I wanted.

Guarding your prophetic word is a must. Your family might not like what God is doing in your life. Your husband might not understand what God is doing in your life. People in the church might not agree with what God is doing in your life.

Others might not like what God is doing in your ministry. This is why you need to keep some things to yourself. Also, some people will try to hinder the blessing of God in your life. YOU MUST BE CAREFUL WHOM YOU SHARE YOUR VISION WITH CONSTANTLY!!

It's in the Seed

You see; everything comes into your life in a seed form. So when you receive a prophetic word, it is released in a seed form. This is another critical reason for guarding your prophetic word. There is an incubation period and a development stage for every prophetic word. You have to watch over your word, so it can come to pass -- God watches over His word to perform it (Jeremiah 1:12).

3. Meditate and Pray Over Your Prophetic Word:

Joshua 1:8 says we are to meditate day and night on the word of God and we will have good success. Psalm 1:2 also says when you meditate on the word day and night you should be like a tree planted by the rivers of water that bringeth forth his fruit in his season; his leaf shall not wither, and whatsoever he doeth shall prosper.

You need to meditate on your prophetic word. Meditate means to mutter; mutter means to speak. If God has greatness in your bowels don't be ashamed to confess it. It is not an arrogant thing to confess it, but it is a God thing.

If God says that you are going to own a business, then agree with the prophetic word and begin to speak it over your life. If God has promised that you are going to be a great intercessor, then confess it. If God said your household is going to be saved, then prophesy to your household. Agree with the prophecy that is pending over your life.

Some people feel embarrassed to agree with what God is doing in their lives. They call this being humble. But being humble does not nullify the purpose and will of God for your life. If God is trying to make you great, agree with Him. You did not come up with the idea, God did. Jeremiah 29:11 says God has an expected end for you. When you have an expectation for the goodness of God to encompass your life, it invites God's presence into your situation.

When people embrace this type of mindset about the purpose and will of God for their lives, it is really false humility. The devil loves to cheat you out of blessings through misguided deceptions. Agree with God and accept your blessings.

Righteous Seed and Generational Blessing

> *Raising up successors or leaving an inheritance for future generations have always been a great concern with God.*

Some blessings that God has ordained for your life are generational blessings; and God has been waiting for a righteous seed to rise up in your family lineage to release the blessings through.

When you study the generations of families in the Old Testament, you will notice that when one or more generation within a family line are wicked, the blessings of God did not flow within that era. It was not that the generational blessings were absent, but there was no righteous seed that God could release the blessings through.

For example the lineage of Hannah: Hannah was righteous and the blessings of God flowed within her life span. Hannah had a son, whose name was Samuel. Samuel was a priest and prophet to the land, so the generational blessings continued to flow. But when Samuel had children, his sons (Joel and Abiah) were wicked (I Samuel 8:2-3). Then the blessings of God were no longer evident.

But when Joel's son was born, Heman, he restored and released the righteous heritage that was held up by the previous generation. He walked in the statutes of the Lord (I Chronicles 6:31-37). Perhaps, some of the blessings you are receiving in your life today are a result of generational blessings.

Raising up successors or leaving an inheritance for future generations have always been a great concern with God. This is why no matter what generation living in each time period, He instructed the children of Israel to teach their children the statues and laws and to always remember it was the Lord that brought their forefathers out of bondage. He wanted them to be raised with the statues and laws of God in their hearts, so that they may grow up and pass this historical data on to the next generation. He wanted them to have an inheritance and a framework and backdrop of the goodness of God that they might forever desire to seek the Lord.

In Proverbs, Chapter 13, Verse 22, it says a good man leaves an inheritance for his children. Again, God is always concerned with the next generation. Generational blessings are always a part of God's blessing plan.

Your Confession Should Line Up With Your Destiny

Your situation should not determine your confession. Pastor Paula White, a renowned 21st century pastor and teacher, says it this way, "All you need to turn your situation around is revelation about your situation." You have to

> *Your present circumstances will always be at odds with your prophetic word.*

confess the word when you don't see anything happening. You have to believe that your prophetic word is working. Your confession must line up with your destiny.

Your present circumstances will always be at odds with your prophetic word. God will speak an encouraging word into your life when you are in your most barren situation. When Abraham was ninety years old, God spoke prophetically into his life that he was going to be a father of many nations. Abraham's wife, Sarah, was barren and they did not have any children. But their present situation did not negate what God wanted to do in his life. This was evidenced when at the age of one hundred, he borne a son.

His and Sarah's natural circumstances were in complete contrast to his prophetic word. The Bible records it this way — "Now Abraham and Sarah were old and well stricken in age..." (Genesis 18:11). However, our time clock is not God's time clock. We are prophetic people, so we must get our directives from the Spirit and not the natural.

Birthing Your Destiny

Meditating and praying over your prophetic word is how you birth your destiny into existence. It is what God did not say in the prophecy that you must obtain or birth in prayer. Remember, people prophesy in part – "For we know in part and we prophesy in part" (I Corinthians 13:9). Plus, anytime you receive a prophecy, you need to be prayerful. Some people prophesy out of zeal and their flesh. The focus of this book; however, is not on false prophecies, but on the authentic ones.

However, never leave it ultimately up to other people to prophesy your destiny in its entirety. Learn how to hear God for yourself. John 10:27 says, "My sheep hear my voice, and I know them, and they follow me." You must learn to

> *When you embrace the destiny of God for your life, it will be governed by two entities: the prophetic and the apostolic.*

recognize God's voice, so that you can follow His directives. This is absolutely essential for God's purpose and destiny to be worked out in your life.

Also, being prayerful will allow you to connect with the people that God has ordained for you to network with in order for your destiny to come to pass. You might have to relocate sometimes. You might have to go through some "stuff." You might have to give up some things. Being prayerful will keep your heart encouraged and keep your mind focused. Meditating and praying over your prophetic word is an essential element in birthing your destiny.

Everyone Has a Predetermined Destiny

Every person on this earth has a prophetic word hovering over his or her life (Ephesians 1:4-5). Before your parents' sperm and egg came together, God had a predetermined destiny for your life. God told Jeremiah in Chapter one and verse five, "Before I formed thee in the belly

I knew thee; and before thou camest forth out of the womb I sanctified thee, and I ordained thee a prophet unto the nations" (Jeremiah 1:5).

If you are a minister now, then you were ordained to be a minister before you were born (Romans 1:1-2). If you are a mother now, then you were destined to be a mother before you were born (Psalm 139:14-15). If you are a pastor now, then you were chosen to be a pastor before you were born (Ephesians 4:11). You are what God says and ordained you to be on this earth.

Your Destiny Has Two Components

When you embrace the destiny of God for your life, it will be governed by two entities: the prophetic and the apostolic. It is the prophetic that gives you clarity and direction about what God wants to do in your life, but it is the apostolic component that gives the prophetic word structure. For example: If you receive a prophetic word that you will be interfacing with kings and dignitaries, then it is the apostolic anointing that teaches you how to govern yourself when you are in their midst.

You see the apostolic ministry is a protocol ministry. It establishes order. We all need government in our lives. How I behave with my "homies" is different than how I behave with millionaires. Don't forget God is a God of order (I Corinthians 14:40).

Favor is a Companion to Purpose

One of the greatest byproducts for birthing and releasing the destiny of God in your life is that favor comes with it. Favor is a companion to purpose. So what, some people won't let you do some things. Just stay in the Will of God and if God has ordained it for your life, then the final decision is not up to them, but God. Favor will get you into places or get you things that others might strive to achieve or attain for years.

This has happened in my life repeatedly. There have been people who shunned me or tried indirectly to block me from getting something. But regardless of all their efforts, God would raise up some people that favored me and I would have immediate access to that which they tried to block. Each time this happened, God removed these individuals out of their positions. I never got angry with them nor did I walk in strife, but God will show you people's hearts. If God has something for you, no devil or no person can stop it. Psalm 41:11 says,

"By this I know that thou favorest me, because mine enemy doth not triumph over me."

Neglect Not The Gift

God wants you not to neglect the gift of God within you. He wants you to stir it up and to give yourself wholly to the purpose and will of God for your life. "Neglect not the gift that is in thee, which was given thee by prophecy, with the laying on of the hands of the presbytery. *Meditate upon these things; give thyself wholly to them; that thy profiting may appear to all."* (1 Timothy 4:14-15)

4. War With Your Prophetic Word:

Why do you need to war with your prophetic word? Because everything in your life can be pointing in the very opposite direction of your prophetic word. You have to continue to declare the word of the Lord over your life even though it looks like nothing is happening. What you see in the natural is not the compass that you should be looking at to determine what God is doing in your life. You should always use your prophetic word to guide you through

> *Your future will not respond to anybody else's voice, but yours.*

the developmental process of your destiny.

Some has said it this way, "Your future will not respond to anybody else's voice, but yours." Your future is created and released through your mouth only. Your future will respond to your voice ONLY. This is why you cannot speak things contrary to your prophetic word because it impedes and hinders the purpose of God from working in your life. So many times we spend much of our life rehearsing the past, but our focus must be on our future and not our past. This is why you must learn to speak to your future instead of your past. Always remember, you cannot retract what you have said, but you can retract what you did not say.[39]

Words Create Your World

Your future is framed and defined by your words, just like God framed the world by His words – "Through faith we understand that the worlds were framed by the word of God" (Hebrews 11:3). Words can change a destiny of a nation and a course of history. Words can be constructive or

> *If you are born again, then you are a prophetic person because you were birthed out of a*

destructive. This is why you must never allow others to create your future for you because they will always create a warped or distorted world for you. One writer wrote, if you allow others to create your world; they will always create it too small.

This is such a true statement. There are blind spots in all of our lives, so when you allow others to dictate your future, you in essence, allow them to create a false future for you. Because it is a false future; then useless effort and energy will be wasted on an unattainable goal. When this occurs, you will feel stressed out and weighted down constantly. The Bible says His mercies are new every day and the blessings of the Lord maketh rich and addeth no sorrow (Proverbs 10:22).

Words Are Containers

Words are containers. Words are connected with the supernatural and the natural. They are infinite. The words you speak today can have a lasting effect on someone throughout his or her life. Whether the words are negative or positive, it will produce some type of fruit. Therefore, you need to monitor the words you speak. Words will either build up or tear down.

If you are born again, then you are a prophetic person because you were birthed out of a prophetic God. I did not say you were a prophet, but because we are birthed out of the loins of God, then we are attached to His infinite nature. Your words have a prophetic affect. It is said that we are the sum total of the words we speak. And as a believer our words have even more of a created power. Never joke about things that could affect your destiny or anybody else's destiny.

Chapter 5

A More Surer Word of Prophecy

Dr. Shirley K. Clark

In the previous sections I have spent a great deal of time talking about prophetic words we received from anointed true vessels of God. But perhaps, you might be in the elite group of people who would say that they have never received a prophetic word from anyone. But whether you have received a prophetic word or not from a preacher, minister or prophet, you still have a more surer word of prophecy and it is the Word of God.

> "We have also a more sure word of prophecy; whereunto ye do well that ye take heed, as unto a light that shineth in a dark place, until that day dawn, and the day star arise in your hearts:
>
> Knowing this first, that no prophecy of the scripture is of any private interpretation.

Discovering Your Destiny

> For the prophecy came not in old time by the will of man: but holy men of God spake as they were moved by the Holy Ghost."
>
> II Peter 1:19-21

Your surer word of prophecy says this about you:
- You are the head and not the tail
- God is your light and your salvation
- No weapon formed against you shall prosper
- God is your refuge and your strength

- The steps of a righteous man are ordered by the Lord
- The Lord is your shepherd and you shall not want
- Greater is He that is in you than he that is in the world
- The Lord is your shield and buckler
- You are blessed going in and blessed going out
- Blessed is the fruit of your womb
- You will be a lender and not a borrower
- God is going to give you houses that you did not build

- You are the seed of Abraham
- Christ has redeemed you from the curse of the law
- But thanks be to God that causes you to triumph in Christ Jesus
- You are bought with a price
- You are a son or daughter of God
- You are redeemed by the blood of Jesus
- Surely goodness and mercy shall follow you all the days of your life

- You are an heir of the Father and a joint-heir of the Son
- You are accepted in the beloved
- You are the apple of God's eyes
- God's banner over you is love
- He that dwelleth in the secret place of the Most High shall abide under the shadow of the Almighty
- You are an overcomer
- You are God's battle ax and weapon of warfare

- Riches and honor are in your house
- You are blessed in the field and blessed in the city
- God has not given you the spirit of fear, but love, power and a sound mind
- A thousand might fall at your side and ten thousand at your right hand, but it shall not come nigh thee
- God will take sickness out of the midst of you
- The wicked flee when no one is chasing them, but you are bold as a lion

- God will hide you in His pavilion
- You can do all things through Christ who strengthens you
- Your God shall supply all your needs according to His riches in glory
- The seven spirits of God are over your life: The Spirit of the Lord, counsel, might, understanding, wisdom, fear of the Lord, knowledge
- He will give you strength when you are faint

- You have eagle's wings
- You have hind's feet
- You are steadfast, unmoveable always abounding in the Word of the Lord
- God delights in your prayers

Then you can begin to war with the Hebrew names of God:

- God I thank you that you are my **Jehovah-Jireh,** the God that supplies all my needs

- God I thank you that you are my **Jehovah-Shalom,** the God of my peace
- God I thank you that you are my **Jehovah-Shammah,** the God who is ever-present
- God I thank you that you are my **Jehovah-Nissi,** the God who is my banner
- God I thank you that you are my **Jehovah-Rohi,** the Lord who is my shepherd
- God I thank you that you are my **Jehovah-**

Tsidkenu, the God who is our righteousness
- God I thank you that you are my **Jehovah-M'kaddesh**, the God who is my sanctifier
- God I thank you that you are my **Jehovah Bore**, the Lord our creator
- God I thank you that you are my **Jehovah-Izuz Weigbbor**, the Lord strong and mighty
- God I thank you that you are my **Jehovah Rophe**, the God that healeth me

- God I thank you that you are my **Jehovah-Makkeh,** the Lord that smiteth
- God I thank you that you are my **Jehovah-Sali**, the Lord my Rock
- God I thank you that you are my **Jehovah-Sabaoth**, the Lord of Hosts
- God I thank you that you are my **Jehovah-Melek**, the Lord is King
- God I thank you that you are my **Jehovah-Shaphat**, the Lord is Judge

- God I thank you that you are my **Jehovah-Maginnenu**, the Lord our defense[40]

Then you can begin to war prophetically about yourself. God I thank you that:
- I am a blessed wife
- I am a blessed mother
- I am a blessed minister of the gospel
- I am a blessed father
- I am a blessed husband
- I am a blessed son
- I am a blessed daughter
- My house is blessed
- My children are blessed

- My family is blessed
- My job is blessed
- My mother is blessed
- My father is blessed
- My sister is blessed
- My brother is blessed
- My husband is blessed
- My wife is blessed
- My church is blessed
- My pastor is blessed

Devil, you cannot curse what God has blessed!!

What the devil meant for evil, God is turning it around for my good.

The Psalmist says "I have been young and I have been old, but I have never seen the righteous forsaken nor his seed begging bread."

It doth not yet appear what you shall be like, but when you see Him, you shall be like Him.
"For we look not at the things that can be seen, but at the things which cannot be seen…"

It's time to war with your prophetic word!!!

When you war with your prophetic word, you are releasing prophetic proclamations within the atmosphere. Therefore, change is inevitable.

Discovering Your Destiny

Dr. Shirley K. Clark

www.ingramcontent.com/pod-product-compliance
Lightning Source LLC
Chambersburg PA
CBHW071912290426
44110CB00013B/1358